What Music!

THE FIFTY-YEAR FRIENDSHIP BETWEEN BEETHOVEN AND NANNETTE STREICHER, WHO BUILT HIS PIANOS

by Laurie Lawlor

Illustrated by Becca Stadtlander

HOLIDAY HOUSE · NEW YORK

In a tall, narrow building on a wide avenue, pianos plinked and plunked day and night. Everyone in quiet Augsburg knew the Stein home.

What music!

Upstairs lived Nannette and her siblings. (She was sixth of fifteen.) The children sang and practiced keyboard turns, trills, chords, and scales. Downstairs in the workshop that smelled of sawdust, fresh lumber, and shellac, craftsmen sawed and hammered, sanded, and painted. Strings quivered. Notes shimmered. Each magnificent instrument had to be tested and tuned before its soundboard was signed with the name Johann Andreas Stein.

Ever since Nannette was tall enough to reach tools on a workbench, she loved to tinker and build. She followed her father everywhere. An unusual man for his time, Stein supported his daughter's talents. She started piano and singing lessons when she was four. Three years later, she played in her first public concert. In 1777, eight-year-old Nannette performed for world-famous musician Wolfgang Amadeus Mozart. Later she was tutored in Latin, French, literature, and mathematics. She continued to spend hours in the workshop, where she learned piano design, construction, and how to run the business.

On a balmy April day in 1787, Ludwig van Beethoven, age seventeen, arrived at Nannette's home. Gawky Ludwig longed to impress Stein, the celebrated piano innovator. Ludwig had not counted on meeting eighteen-year-old Nannette or her happy family (so different from his own). Take a seat, they said. Play something.

Ludwig did what he loved best. He trusted his imagination and wove together themes of joy and sadness, rage and hope.

What music!

As he played, he forgot about his drunken father, dying mother, and needy younger brothers back at their impoverished home in Bonn. He forgot about his disappointing trip to Vienna to beg an audience before Mozart. He concentrated on making the piano sing.

Bravo! Bravo!

His performance undoubtedly impressed Nannette, who'd grown up around some of the finest musicians in Europe. Of course, Ludwig knew he was stupendous. Modesty was never one of his virtues.

Unlike Nannette, Ludwig had a hardscrabble childhood. He was the eldest of four children raised by a cheerless mother. At an early age, tiny Ludwig stood on tiptoe on a footstool to play the keyboard.

His first music teacher was his father, a court-appointed singer. If five-year-old Ludwig didn't follow directions, his father boxed his ears, rapped his fingers, or locked him in the cellar. The woods became Ludwig's refuge.

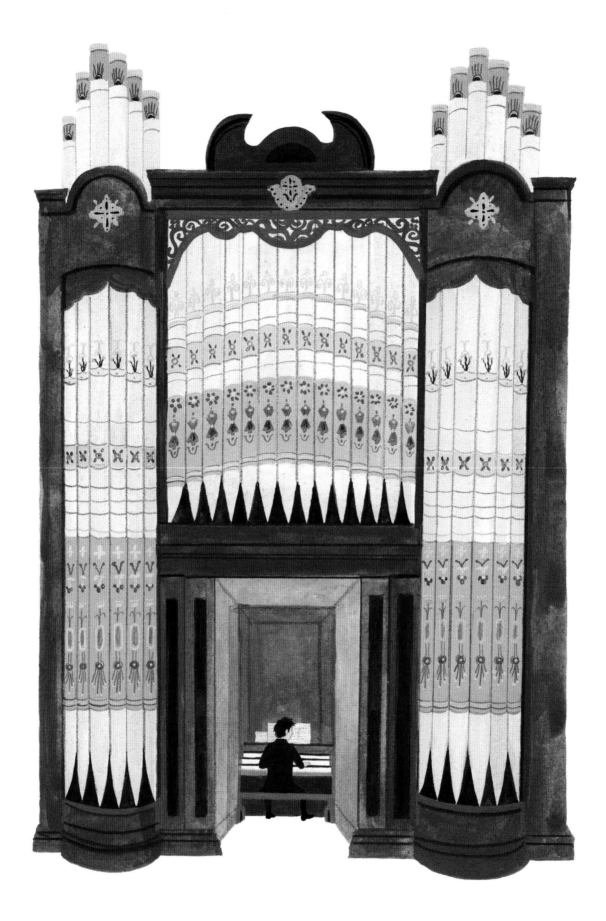

After a hodgepodge of short-term instructors, Ludwig finally found a long-term coach who insisted he study *The Well-Tempered Clavier* by composer Johann Sebastian Bach. Ludwig quit school at eleven to make money as an organist's assistant. He never mastered spelling, multiplication, or legible handwriting. Luckily, he became an avid reader. Ludwig joined a local orchestra. At fourteen, he worked from morning till night as an accompanist for church services, theatrical rehearsals, and opera performances. After his mother and infant sister died in 1787, his father's drunk and disorderly charges cost him his job and threatened to land him in jail. By the time Ludwig was seventeen, he'd become the main breadwinner in the family.

In background and personality, Nannette and Ludwig were as opposite as fast and slow, loud and soft, high and low. Ludwig liked jokes and puns, but he could be headstrong, prone to anger, and prickly when criticized. Proper Nannette preferred an orderly life, yet she had a lively way of speaking, a "cheerfully open" manner, and tender empathy for other people. Despite their differences, they became friends.

What they shared was an ambitious dream that someday the piano could be a powerful solo instrument capable of making music as perfect as a palmful of wild raspberries.

In 1792, the fathers of Ludwig and Nannette died. Ludwig set off to seek musical fame in Vienna, the glittering capital of Austria and home to nearly 300 pianists and 6,000 piano students. Because she was a woman, Nannette was not permitted by law to take over the piano workshop even though she was the most experienced person in her family. She had to partner with her teenage brother. A dozen journeymen continued to work for *Geschwister Stein*—Stein Brother and Sister.

In 1794, Nannette married Johann Andreas Streicher and took his last name. A musician and amateur composer, he became the male "front" who managed the finances, marketing, and correspondence. Nannette remained the brains behind piano design and production.

In a bold move that year, she moved the business by Danube River barge to Vienna. By 1802, she and her brother went separate ways. For the first time, she proudly signed her own pianos, *Nannette Streicher née Stein a Vienne*—Nannette Stein Streicher in Vienna. The thriving business would move three more times—always to bigger quarters.

Meanwhile, Ludwig had become a wild-man celebrity in Vienna concert halls. After years of formal, polite music making, wealthy audiences wanted something revolutionary: an emotional, unconventional pianist who performed "duels" with other musicians. Amazed listeners cheered Ludwig's symphonies, concertos, songs, piano sonatas—and, later, his opera. Publishers printed and sold his works as quickly as he produced them.

Like a modern experimental pilot on a quest for a jet that could go higher, faster, farther, Ludwig sought a piano that could meet his soaring expectations. Give me something stronger with a wider range of expression and bigger volume, he told Nannette. More keys. More strings.

What Ludwig wanted was a piano as expressive as a human voice and as varied in tone and timbre as an entire orchestra combined. As Ludwig's fame grew, so did the importance of his piano endorsements.

Inspired by Ludwig's suggestions, Nannette plunged into major design changes to keep the piano's clarity and subtle sounds while increasing volume. She tripled the number of strings, boosted the number of keys, and strengthened construction to withstand pounding of string-breaking virtuosos like Ludwig. A few models even offered special effects like sounds of drums, bells, cymbals, bassoons, and lutes. Soon Streicher pianos were among the largest, loudest, most spectacular pianos in Europe. While running a thriving workshop, Nannette took care of a daughter and three sons born between 1794 and 1801. The youngest had "Ludwig" as his middle name.

The business produced more than 600 pianos between 1810 and 1815. To encourage music appreciation and sales, Nannette and her husband offered free concerts in a 300-seat concert hall. Statues of famous composers stared down from the walls, including scowling Ludwig. He rented, played, and borrowed more than a dozen different pianos from Nannette's workshop throughout his life. He confided that since 1809, "I have always specially preferred them."

At Ludwig's performances audience members swooned and cheered. Then disaster struck.

When he was only twenty-eight, he noticed an odd "fizzling and sizzling" in his ears. Earaches plagued him. Soon he could barely understand friends' conversations or singers' performances. He tried every doctor, every cure. Nothing worked.

In a society that treated the hearing impaired as second-class citizens, he feared having his growing deafness discovered. Who would hire a concert pianist who could not hear? How would he write music? Ludwig struggled to pretend everything was fine.

In 1802 he collapsed from exhaustion after rehearsing, conducting, performing, and composing with what hearing he had left. His doctor sent him to the country to rest for six months. Surrounded by woods and mountains, Ludwig decided he must change his life. He would no longer hide his deafness. He'd use his suffering to write music to help other people. He gave up performing and focused on composing.

During the next three decades, he went deeper into the music he heard in his "mind's ear" to create sonatas and entire symphonies. His boundary-breaking work would forever change the world of music.

Throughout these especially difficult years, Nannette's friendship remained a crucial lifeline. He moved 67 times in 35 years and was often her neighbor in Vienna.

One summer, a visitor sat at the piano in Nannette's home puzzling out one of Ludwig's works. Just as they'd reached the last movement, Ludwig appeared, leaned over the piano still holding his "ear trumpet," and demonstrated the right notes on the keyboard. Then he disappeared. Nannette wasn't the least surprised. Ludwig was such a frequent visitor at her home, he was like a member of the family. Her guest, however, was shocked to see the musical superstar in person.

Nannette profoundly respected Ludwig and his music, which she played expertly throughout her life. She was honest about his faults. In later years, she compared him to a bear "sulky and froward." Once, because of his ragged clothes and crazy hair, police mistakenly arrested him as a street beggar. His loud laughter sounded like a scream. He often insulted passersby, and when he shook hands, he nearly crushed fingers.

To Ludwig, Nannette remained "Beloved Friend," the one person who inspired "an uncommonly good influence." Her support proved crucial in 1818, when his personal life and household chaos nearly overwhelmed him. Somehow he managed to sketch in his notebook the rough idea that would become one of his most spectacular symphonies. Little by little, he envisioned a groundbreaking work with a massive chorus and soloists to sing his adaptation of "Ode to Joy" by poet Friedrich Schiller.

Word of the revolutionary symphony spread like wildfire. On May 7, 1824, an excited crowd—undoubtedly including Nannette—packed the theatre. Three conductors graced the stage, including Ludwig. Profoundly deaf, he had the role of honorary maestro.

The Ninth Symphony's opening fanfare sounded like the world falling apart. Then the music rose along a suspenseful arc to the electrifying moment when the chorus finally stood. They sang "Ode to Joy," a rallying cry for all humanity to experience happiness and unite—freed from fear, oppression, and corrupt tyrants.

What music!

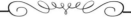

Giddy with emotion, the audience leapt to their feet. They applauded, waved hats and handkerchiefs, and demanded five curtain calls.

Ludwig, who had his back to the crowd, did not notice the Ninth Symphony's emotional impact. Finally, a young woman pulled on his sleeve, prompting him to turn around. His response? Unusual stoic calm.

One spring day in 1824, Nannette and her husband stopped to visit Ludwig on their way to a country vacation. Using a notebook and pen to communicate, Nannette expressed delight in a shared memory. Did Ludwig recall how as a teenager he had played her father's piano? And now, years later, he experienced firsthand the pianos made by her grown son and working partner. Clearly, Nannette was proud that her hard-won enterprise had stayed in her family.

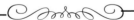

After a lingering illness, Ludwig died March 26, 1827. Three days later, Nannette stood in the courtyard outside Ludwig's home, where the coffin was placed before the funeral cortege made its way to the cemetery. Nearly 20,000 people lined the streets for the grandest funeral Vienna had ever given a commoner.

What music!

Nannette died January 16, 1833. She was buried in St. Marx Cemetery. Eventually her grave and that of her son and husband were relocated to the Vienna Central Cemetery, close to that of her friend, Ludwig van Beethoven.

AUTHOR'S NOTE
Looking for Clues of a Friendship

According to church baptism records, Ludwig van Beethoven was born December 26, 1770—a date that his father sometimes changed to make him appear a younger musical prodigy. On January 2, 1769, Anna Maria Stein (nicknamed "Nannette") was born.

Countless letters, paintings, statues, coins, medallions, musical scores, journals, contracts, and diaries featuring world-famous Beethoven have endured. Everything from locks of his hair and ear trumpets to pocket watches and spectacles (and even a death mask) have been preserved in museums. There are an estimated 300,000 Beethoven books, articles, films, and recordings.

Artifacts from Nannette Streicher's personal and professional life are rare. In Austria of the eighteenth and nineteenth centuries, few women succeeded in designing pianos. Fewer still could command the loyalty of a skilled staff made up entirely of men who belonged to exclusive, ironclad guilds. While she was pulling off this remarkable feat, she was also raising a family. Amazingly, she was able to hand down the business to her son, Johann Baptist, who passed it along to Nannette's grandson, Emil Streicher. Her husband, while a close and trusted confidant, never had shares in the piano-building enterprise.

I was inspired to investigate the friendship between Ludwig and Nannette when I discovered more than 60 letters and notes penned between 1817 and 1818. These were all addressed to Nannette. None of her replies survived. Before the invention of text messaging or telephones, Ludwig's left-handed scrawl offers glimpses into his life and that of Nannette. (She was the only woman with whom he had such a long, enduring friendship.) Who was she?

The letters—often delivered by Nannette's daughter, Sophie—provided a fascinating look at the great composer and Nannette. Some letters had musical jokes and puns. Others were requests for help finding listening devices or "hearing trumpets" to magnify sounds. He begged that she retrofit a piano "to accommodate my poor hearing, and to make it as powerful as is humanly possible." He complained about his bad health. He borrowed money. He asked for advice about honest housekeepers, decent cooks, grocery bills, and where to buy spoons and how to get his laundry done. (Had she seen his missing socks?)

I wish we could hear her responses.

Ludwig never married. In 1815 he attempted to adopt his young nephew, Karl. In his letters, he cajoled Nannette to help him put his upside-down household in order. She did her best. However, Ludwig's struggle to create a family did not work out the way he hoped. Karl ran away to his mother and a custody battle began. When many friends abandoned Ludwig during years of strife, Nannette and her husband tried their best to help him.

A treasure trove of recorded insights are "Conversation Books" that Ludwig began using in 1818 because of his deafness. Acquaintances, family, and friends like Nannette wrote their side of conversations while he spoke aloud. He carried notebooks on long walks and visits to homes, coffee houses, and cafes. Sometimes he scribbled notes to himself: grocery lists, musical ideas, newspaper advertisements. More than 140 surviving notebooks are being footnoted and translated into English.

Nannette Streicher's Enduring Legacy

The most revealing artifacts about Nannette are her pianos. Of the estimated 1,000 she built in her lifetime, only forty have survived in private collections and museums around the world. The last spectacular mahogany piano to bear the inscription *Nannette Streicher née Stein a Vienne* was built in 1823 for King George IV of England.

Nannette's legacy continues thanks to the work of two remarkable American craftswomen. Margaret F. Hood researched and worked on a replica of Streicher's 1816 masterpiece. Anne Acker finished building the piano following Hood's premature death in 2008.

The two friends shared an abiding love of music and early stringed keyboard instruments. Both were inspired and motivated by the story of Nannette Streicher.

Hood, an accomplished painter and equestrian, became fascinated by early instrument building in the 1960s and founded a company to create fortepianos in Wisconsin in 1976. She became an important mentor to Acker, a devoted pianist who had also trained in mathematics and computer science. With two small children at home (she used half the basement playroom as her workshop), she began building and repairing harpsicords and antique pianos—a passion that turned into her own business, repairing, playing, and building early keyboard instruments in Pennsylvania and Georgia.

Acker bought the unfinished reproduction from Wood's husband. Using her friend's extensive research and photographs, Acker was determined to complete the "giant jigsaw puzzle" of parts and pieces. "I loved the idea that a woman built a piano, another woman researched and started building the replica, and a third finished it." Acker completed this dream in 2019 with the debut of the Streicher piano at the Boston Early Music Festival Exhibition—just in time for the 250th anniversary of Nannette Streicher's birthday.

Nannette Streicher has been an inspiration for Acker from the moment she heard of her. "She managed a family, an important business, and designed and refined the instruments at a time when women who worked in various industries were faceless in the background, names forgotten to history." For Acker, who balanced family and a career in male-dominated fields, Streicher was "truly a genius and a modern woman ahead of her time."

Both Acker and Streicher shared an early fascination with playing the piano, starting lessons at age four. Both had supportive fathers who encouraged their skills and their entrance into fields controlled mostly by men. Acker marvels at Streicher's ability to think in three dimensions, understand how wood quality effects sound, and maximize leverages—the angle and force needed to hit a string in such a way that it creates a musical tone. "She made instruments that were both delicate yet strong."

The process of creating a musical instrument from materials as simple as wood, wire, glue, and leather fills Acker with wonder. "You have all these pieces all over the floor, and as you work, you start to put them together. Then one day, you have this big part finished and wow, it's beautiful."

Beethoven's Ninth Symphony:
Overcoming Adversity, Finding Triumph

During his lifetime, Ludwig created 32 piano sonatas, 16 string quartets, 10 sonatas for violin and piano, 7 piano trios, 5 sonatas for cello and piano, 2 masses, 9 symphonies—and assorted other works. Altogether he composed 720 pieces of music.

Among his most universally recognized is his Ninth Symphony.

He managed to finish this while ill and reeling from the disastrous adoption of his nephew. He never gave up. In 1818, he first sketched the idea in his notebook: "Adagio Cantique. A symphonic song of piety in the old mode."

The Ninth Symphony's production required an enormous assembly of instrumentalists (24 violins and double winds), extra timpani, and a battalion of singers. The symphony's debut on May 7, 1824, almost never happened. Copyists rushed to finish creating by hand the massive score. Up until the last minute, Ludwig and the organizers squabbled over the venue, the ticket price, and securing conductors, soloists, orchestra, and chorus.

Yet the Ninth Symphony was a tremendous success.

In addition to rave reviews, publishers printed portraits of Ludwig in free newspapers—like today's pop-star posters. Ludwig, however, made scant payment for his pathbreaking work.

What was it about this symphony that gripped the first Viennese audience? In the aftermath of endless wars, diseases, and economic disasters in Europe, people were exhausted. The bloody twenty-year Napoleonic Wars that began in 1802 were a relentless, global conflict. Now people longed for peace. They longed for happiness. They longed for the ideal of brotherhood.

What may seem remarkable is that 54-year-old Ludwig van Beethoven, a man who had experienced so little joy in his own life, created a monumental work celebrating humankind's triumph over isolation and loneliness. His music still speaks powerfully to us today.

HISTORICAL FIGURES MENTIONED IN THIS BOOK

Wolfgang Amadeus Mozart (1756–1791) was an Austrian composer, conductor, pianist, organist, and violinist whose vast body of work influenced Beethoven's early compositions. Some of his most famous pieces are the *Jupiter Symphony* and *The Magic Flute,* an opera.

Johann Sebastian Bach (1688–1750) was a prolific German composer and celebrated harpsichordist, organist, violist, and violinist. Some of his most famous compositions are the *Brandenburg Concertos* and *The Well-Tempered Clavier,* a collection of works created to teach keyboard, but which are now often performed.

Friedrich Schiller (1759–1805) was a German dramatist, philosopher, and one of Beethoven's favorite poets. He is most famous for his philosophical ideas and for his plays, including *William Tell* and *The Robbers.*

BIBLIOGRAPHY

BEETHOVEN

Anderson, Emily, ed. *The Letters of Beethoven*, Vol. I–III. (NY: St. Martin's Press, 1961).

Caeyers, Jan. *Beethoven, A Life.* (Oakland, CA: University of California Press, 2020).

Clive, Peter. *Beethoven and His World.* (Oxford, England: Oxford University Press, 2001).

Hamburger, Michael, ed. *Beethoven: Letters and Conversations.* (London: Thames and Hudson, 1951).

Matthews, Denis. *Beethoven Piano Sonatas.* (London: BBC Music Guides, 1967).

Morris, Edmund. *Beethoven: the Universal Composer.* (NY: HarperCollins, 2005).

Siepmann, Jeremy. *Beethoven: His Life and Music.* (Naperville, IL: Sourcebooks, 2006).

Swafford, Jan. *Beethoven: Anguish and Triumph.* (NY: Houghton Mifflin, 2014).

STREICHER/STEIN

Donhauser, Peter and Alexander Langer. *Streicher der Drei Generationen Klavierbau in Wien.* (Kolm: Verlag Christoph Dohr, 2014).

Ehmer, Josef. "Family and business among master artisans and entrepreneurs: The case of 19th Century Vienna," *History of the Family* 6 (2001) p. 187–202.

Fuller, Richard A. "Andreas Streicher's Notes on the fortepiano." *Early Music.* November 1984, p. 461–470.

Hughes, Rosemary, ed. *Mozart Pilgrimage, Being the Travel Diaries of Vincent and Mary Novello in the Year 1829.* (London: Eulenburg Books, 1955).

Kopitz, Klaus Martin. "Nannette Streicher," Musik and Gender im Internet. Hamburg: 2011.

Latcham, Michael. "Development of the Streicher Firm of Piano Builders under the leadership of Nannette Streicher, 1792 to 1823," *Das Wiener Klavier Bis 1850.* Ed. by Darmstaddter, Beatrix.

p. 43–71. Tutzing: Hans Schneider, 2007. Kunst Historicshces Museum.

Latcham, Michael, ed. Translator. Vol. I. *The Notebooks of Johann Andreas Stein.* (Florian Noetzel Verlag: Heinrichshoven Books, 2014).

Latcham, Michael. *Pianos for Haydn, Mozart and Beethoven: Change and Contrast.* (Bloomington: Indiana University Press, 2016).

Rollett, Hermann. *Beethoven in Baden.* (Wien: Carl Gerold's Sons, 1902).

Skowroneck, Tilman. "Andreas Streicher and Piano Building," *Early Keyboard Journal*, Vol. 30. (Ramsey: Southeastern Historical Keyboard Society, Midwest Historical Keyboard Society, 2013). P. 54.

Wiesner, Merry E. *Working Women in Renaissance Germany.* (New Brunswick, NJ: Rutgers University Press, 1986).

Wosnitzka, Susanne. "Music HERstory: Nannette Streicher." Donne365 Women Composers 365 Days a Year. https://donne365.blogspot.com/2020/01/music-herstory-nannette-streicher

VIENNA

Barea, Ilsa. *Vienna Legend and Reality.* (London: Secker and Warburg, 1966).

Johnson, William M. *Vienna: The Golden Age 1815–1914.* (NY: Clarkson N. Potter, Inc., Crown, 1980).

Wangermann, Ernst. *The Austrian Achievement 1700–1800.* (NY: Harcourt Brace Jovanovich, Inc., 1973).

MOZART

Lady Wallace, ed. *Letters of Wolfgang Amadeus Mozart*, Vol. I (Philadelphia: Hurd & Houghton, 1866).

PIANO BUILDING

Badura-Skoda, Eva. *18th Century Fortepiano Grand and Its Patrons.* (Indianapolis: Indiana University Press, 2017).

Barron, James. *Piano: The Making of a Steinway Concert Grand.* (NY: Henry Holt, Times Books, 2006).

Chapin, Miles, and Rodica Prato. *88 Keys: The Making of a Steinway Piano.* (NY: Crown, 1997).

Harding, Rosamond E.M. T*he Piano-Forte: Its History Traced to the Great Exhibition of 1851.* (Surrey, England: Gresham Books, 1978).

Isacoff, Stuart. *A Natural History of the Piano.* (NY: Alfred Knopf, 2011).

SOURCE NOTES

Page 16   "cheerfully open"   Rollet, Hermann. *Beethoven in Baden.* (Wein: Carl Gerold's Sons, 1902). P. 23.

Page 23   "I have . . . them."   Anderson, Emily, ed. *Letters of Beethoven*, Vol. II. (NY: St. Martin's Press, 1961). P. 686.

Page 25   "fizzling and sizzling"   Caeyers, Jan. *Beethoven, A Life.* (Oakland: University of California Press, 2020). P. 169.

Page 28   "It took . . . again."   Kopitz, Klaus Martin. "Nannette Streicher," Musik and Gender im Internet. Hamburg: 2011, P. 5.

Page 30   "sulky and froward"   Hughes, Rosemary, ed. *Mozart Pilgrimage, Being the Travel Diaries of Vincent and Mary Novello in the Year 1829.* (London: Eulenburg Books, 1955). P. 966.

Page 30 "Beloved Friend" and "an . . . influence." Anderson, Emily, ed. *The Letters of Beethoven*, Vol. II. (NY: St. Martin's Press, 1961). Pp. 685–6; 734.

Page 40 "to accommodate . . . possible." Ibid. P. 785.

Page 42 "Adagio . . . mode."   Caeyers, Jan. *Beethoven, A Life.* (Oakland: University of California Press, 2020). P. 488.

For Jack —L.L.
For Davey and Laura —B.S.

The publisher would like to thank harpsichordist and composer Asako Hirabayashi
for vetting the musical instruments in the art in this book for authenticity.

HOLIDAY HOUSE is registered in the U.S. Patent and Trademark Office.
Printed in bound in June 2023 at Leo Paper, Heshan, China.
The artwork was created using gouache and colored pencil.
www.holidayhouse.com
1 3 5 7 9 10 8 6 4 2

Library of Congress Cataloging-in-Publication Data

Names: Lawlor, Laurie, author. | Stadtlander, Becca, illustrator.
Title: What music : the fifty-year friendship between Beethoven and
Nannette Streicher, who built his pianos / by Laurie Lawlor ;
illustrated by Becca Stadtlander.
Description: [First edition.] | New York : Holiday House, 2023. | Includes
bibliographical references. | Audience: Ages 6–9 | Audience: Grades 2–3
Summary: "This picture book biography chronicles the lifelong
friendship that began in adolescence between Ludwig van Beethoven and
master piano maker Nannette Streicher emphasizing her support for him
and his work and his influence on the many innovations she made to piano
Construction"—Provided by publisher.
Identifiers: LCCN 2022014956 | ISBN 9780823451432 (hardcover)
Subjects: LCSH: Beethoven, Ludwig van, 1770-1827—Juvenile literature.
Streicher, Nannette, 1769-1833—Juvenile literature.
Composers—Austria—Biography—Juvenile literature. | Piano
makers—Austria—Biography—Juvenile literature.
Classification: LCC ML3930.B4 L38 2023 | DDC 780.92/2
[B]—dc23/eng/20220331
LC record available at https://lccn.loc.gov/2022014956

ISBN: 978-0-8234-5143-2 (hardcover)

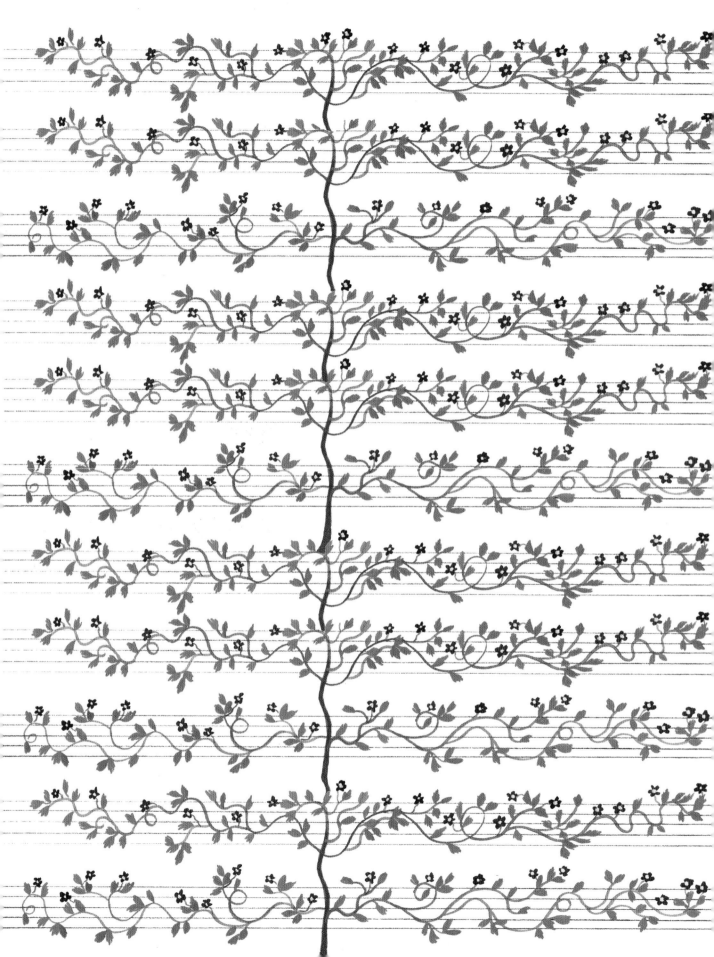